Strategies for Investment Success

Tips and practical advice for starting, growing, and managing your property portfolio

Julie Condliffe

LEVITICAL ORDER

PUBLISHING, INC
Since 2014
London, England

Library of Congress Cataloging-in-Publication Data

Julie Condliffe
Strategies for Investment Success
ISBN 978-1547266999

Published by Levitical Order, Inc
London, England

Printed in London, United Kingdom
All Rights Reserved ©2017 Julie Condliffe, Levitical Order, Inc

Dedicated to my dearest mother
Monica Masanzu

Introduction

Welcome to Strategies for Investment Success, a blueprint for navigating the U.K.'s property investment sector!

As an experienced property litigation solicitor, I have spent over 15 years working on cases involving property dispute resolution. In addition to this, I've also spent the last ten years amassing my own portfolio. I've invested in a mix of commercial and residential properties, and have learnt valuable lessons along the way – some of the most important of which I'm about to share with you.

Inside this book, there are tips for adopting a winning mindset and developing a strategy that will help you see maximum returns on your investments. This is especially important when starting out if you are a new property investor. I'm hoping to help you shave years off your learning curve and avoid mistakes that I learned myself by trial and error.

We will discuss everything from tenant screening to property staging, where and how to find great deals, financing acquisition, buy-to-let versus fix and flip, property management do's and don'ts and many other important aspects of investment. These may be unfamiliar terms to you right now. But they are not as complicated as they sound, and they will soon become a very familiar part of your life.

The UK's private rental sector has experienced a boom in recent years, with the buy-to-let market becoming increasingly buoyant. Doubtless, Brexit will have an impact on the property market.

Whether you're a novice investor or are looking to generate more profit from an existing portfolio, my passion for property alongside my expertise in real estate law enables me to provide some guidance that can help you at any stage in your journey.

My personal journey began in my home country of Zimbabwe, a place I left in search of a better life. The youngest of eight children, I grew up in Harare. My father died when I was ten months old. He was a bus driver shot in the war of liberation. Soon after his death, we were forced to leave our rural village, becoming for all intents and purposes homeless. My dearest mum who had just lost her beloved husband had to deal with the rejection and the eviction.

I was only ten months old at the time, so I cannot tell you how she felt. I can only imagine that had the blood from her bleeding heart been measured, it would have flooded rivers.

We had no access to housing benefits or any governmental support, and while our mum did the best for us, it was still a struggle.

After being kicked out of the village, my mum moved to Harare. She managed to secure a job as a housemaid for a very kind Englishwoman we affectionately called "Aunt Maggie." Aunt Maggie was very kind to us. She allowed us the privilege of having some of the old clothes that her children and grandchildren could not fit anymore. Those were the best clothes we had. We wore those mainly to church on Sundays.

As a little child, I remember running to school early in the morning with no shoes on. Mum invested all the money she had on us to get an education. Shoes and decent clothes were a luxury. Mum knew and helped us understand that the greatest investment is in education and knowledge.

Before school almost every morning, we had to go the farmyard to help till the land, plough and harvest the crops ("kumunda") depending on the season.

Aunt Maggie gave us accommodation in the form of a ramshackle house, which we were tremendously grateful for. The house (if I can call it that), had one bedroom. We used a bedsheet to divide the bedroom into two bedrooms. My two brothers shared a room, and the seven of us girls (including my mum) shared the other room.

While the circumstances I grew up in were unenviable; we were a happy family. We lived in the present and enjoyed every little thing life brought our way. As we didn't have electricity, we could not read at nighttime. Instead, Mum told us all enjoyable tales before bedtime, which we looked forward to. Each tale had a hidden moral to empower us. The key lessons being believing in yourself; the power of setting goals, and the benefits of giving and helping others.

As the only thing that divided our rooms was the makeshift curtain, we could all laugh together and tell jokes before bed. We were, and still are, a close-knit family.

Regardless of our circumstances, Mum always helped us believe that there was more to us than our current circumstances. She instilled in me a belief system that helped me understand that the only limitations are those that I place on myself. She helped me understand that my circumstances do not define me and that I had to look beyond them.

In addition to working as a housemaid for Aunt Maggie, Mum also sought other ways to make ends meet. She would go to the clothes factory and pick up all the cuttings from clothes: the little pieces of material thrown away. She would sew them up together to make bedding for us. After a while, she started selling the bedding to other families. She also started knitting doily crochet, which she ended up exporting to South Africa. My mother's resourcefulness was taxing on her, but it became quite profitable. We got to a stage where we could go to school wearing proper uniforms and shoes!

Years later, Mum was now able to get us better accommodation. Aunt Maggie persuaded Mum to stay, on the agreement that she would sell the ramshackle property we lived into Mum, together with two acres of the land to enable my mother to build a house for us. This was excellent. The agreement was that Mum would forfeit her wages for five years and then the land would be hers.

Mum fulfilled her end of the bargain. She had to work extremely hard on her side, and hustle to be able to look after us. She worked tirelessly to pursue her dream of owning a property. As a woman of integrity, she worked just as hard, if not harder, to fulfill her obligations under the contract.

On expiration of the five-year period, Aunt Maggie confirmed that Mum now owned the property. What an incredible moment! We were all ecstatic! Though she wasn't exactly jumping up and down, she was joyously singing her Catholic songs.

A year later, Aunt Maggie passed away. Her children denied the existence of the agreement. We had no paperwork to prove it; no leg to stand on. They got some of the best lawyers in the land to argue their case. We had no chance of winning. We could hardly afford a lawyer. I cannot begin to tell you how we felt. Can you imagine how Mum felt? Déjà vu.

I had always watched the television programme "Ally

McBeal" through Aunty Maggie's window. I knew I wanted to be a lawyer. This incident cemented this desire. I became firm in my resolution to become a lawyer. It had now become imperative. No matter what, I resolved that I would bring justice to the world. My passion for property was set alight. My passion for justice; justice in property.

I wanted to become a lawyer. A property lawyer. I was gutted when I could not make it to the local university. We only had one university in Zimbabwe at the time. The UK was my second option. So, I headed to the UK.

The farewell at the airport was heart-rending. We all tried to be strong for each other, but you could see the occasional teardrop. I was wretched as soon as I got onto the airplane. I sobbed inconsolably. Had I made the right decision? Would I ever see my family again? What if I didn't? Should I go back? Was it too late? So many questions. The fear, the pain, the doubt.

After take-off, I knew there was no turning back. Literally. I had to regroup. I reminded myself of the primary driving force behind my departure. I was the change I needed. I was the change my family hungered for. I resolved to face whatever was before me valiantly.

My mother and the remainder of my siblings clubbed together and gave me £500 to start my journey. When I arrived, I knew no one in the UK. I needed to get to Victoria Station and then take the tube to North London to someone who was known to my sister.

I performed mental gymnastics trying to figure out what this "tube" would look like. Little did I know that it was simply an underground train. As you rightly imagined, I got lost a few times before I arrived in North London. The key thing is: I arrived.

I had so many mixed emotions. The prospect of a better future for my family and I was exhilarated. The fear of the unknown was equally debilitating.

On arrival in North London, my sister's friend was quite welcoming. At least, for a couple of days. On day three, late in the night, I was told I had to leave quickly as the Home Office was visiting the property. I was half asleep. I had neither the inclination nor the right to argue. I was lawfully in this country. Therefore, I shouldn't have been affected by the alleged visit. Anyway, I left. I had to.

Dragging my little black suitcase along, I fled into the deep, dark, ice-cold night. I had only been in dear England for two winter days. I was still trying to warm up to the slicing cold weather.

I had nowhere to go. I caught the next bus heading anywhere. I had to go somewhere. Where though? Where would I go?

Soon – or so it seemed – the bus driver reminded me that we were at the bus station and that this was the last stop. I aimlessly crawled off the bus.

Reality hit home. I had no home. I had nowhere to sleep. I was dumbstruck with terror. I was homeless in a foreign country. I had anticipated challenges, but not in this fashion. I paced up and down the street. Troubled. Desperate.

As I passed a red telephone booth, I just had that sinking feeling that that was going to be my home. At least for tonight. And yes, it was. I had no option.

It was a tight squeeze for my little suitcase and me even as a tiny size eight (I hasten to add – at the time). It was cold. I was frightened. I imagined every possible negative thing happening to me: abduction, rape, murder – the list goes on. I prayed. I prayed really hard. I sang. I shivered. I prayed again. I sang. I cried. The song I sang the most was: "God will make a way when there seems to be no way. He works in ways we cannot see. He will make a way for me. He will be my guide." I would recite Psalms 91 and pray again. Every time I dozed off, my head would bash the metal phone in the booth as a gentle reminder of where I was. As if I would forget!

On two occasions, people came to use the payphone. On the first occasion, I spoke out loud pretending there was someone on the other end of the phone. I then said my pretend goodbyes and let the gentleman use the phone. I walked around the corner and slid back unnoticed (or so I hoped) when he had finished.

On the later occasion, I was too tired even to pretend I was talking. I simply walked out and stood outside the booth almost as if I was marking my territory. As soon as the lady finished using the phone, I walked right back in and reclaimed my uncomfortable, but less windy accommodation.

I continued to shiver hysterically; inwardly from fear and externally from the harsh cold. Even in that dark, dreary cold night, I knew that a brighter day would come. I knew that there was a brighter future ahead. I had to press on. I remembered that ramshackle house. I remembered the pain that we as a family had gone through. I reminded myself that my goals were not an option, they were not a preference, they were a MUST. I had to achieve. I had to go through whatever I needed to go through to achieve my goals. While quitting was tempting, it wasn't an option.

Was that a glimmer of dawn I could see? Yes, it was the break of dawn. The break of dawn gave hope. The hope of a better life.

I could tell no one of my vagabond experience. Everyone back home was looking up to me to change their lives – how can you tell someone who is counting on you to create a better life that you're homeless? How can you tell them that the land of milk and honey is not as fresh as they think? God and my belief system helped me to press on even through my darkest hours.

Fast forward a little while later, I started university and worked hard (I studied nursing as it was the only course that would allow me a bursary and free accommodation. I felt a bit guilty about it, but it was the only course that would allow me what I required.

Every day after university, I would go to work at McDonald's. At least three nights a week, after my shift I would go to the local care home to do a night shift. This went on for a few years. I effectively had no social life. This helped me send money home and start saving for my future law degree – and to eventually buy a property.

It paid off.

My sacrifice and hard work helped me look after my family. I saved enough money to bring some of my family to England. My mother also managed to visit me a few times before she died. She died a happy woman. Life got better for us as a family. The money I saved helped me to do my law training eventually and to start my investment journey.

I believe you can do anything if you set your mind to it. You have to have the right belief system.

Making a profit through investment takes planning, practice, and expertise, and it's my hope that with this book, you can pick up some valuable, usable tips that can help turn your dreams into a (prosperous) reality!

I was a novice, scared of figures, and anxious of getting things wrong. But with hard work and determination, I still succeeded. If I can do it, I know you can do so too.

~ Julie

Contents

"AIM INTO A VOID,
AND YOU'LL HIT NOTHING
EVERY TIME"
— JULIE CONDLIFFE

Goal Power

Why do you want to invest?

It seems a simple enough question to answer, and for most of us, the answer will be the same – to make money.

But while that may be the first answer that springs to mind, there's often a deeper reason behind it. For example, many people want to generate income from investing in property to escape the rat race and earn a means in a way that doesn't involve sitting behind a desk from 9-5. For others, it may be a case of creating a second income stream to put children through university or private tuition. Some may build a property portfolio as part of their estate planning or retirement strategy; some may invest to create a business, while for others, it's simply a means of extra pocket money. Whatever the reasons, it's important to define your goals and have a clear idea of what you want to achieve.

Why? Because property investment isn't always smooth sailing (...more on that later).

Mistakes are inevitable, and challenges are more or less guaranteed, and without any targets or end goals, jumping these hurdles can prove incredibly difficult. What's more, when times get tough and morale drops, having clearly defined goals to return to will help you through the difficult patches. You remember how I struggled when I became homeless. It was the goals that I had set for myself that gave me the resolve to soldier on despite the hardships I encountered. Without these to think about, being faced with troublesome properties or difficult tenants may be enough to make you want to give up completely. You cannot underestimate the power of having clearly defined goals. Goal power!

Before going any further, take some time to generate some goals. Write them down. I set short-term goals and long-term goals. In setting short-term goals, I consider where I want to be within 12 months. I then set five-year goals and determine where I want to be in ten years' time. I evaluate areas that are most important to me and set specific goals for each of those areas e.g. family; finances; career, and personal development. I consider exactly what I want to achieve in those specific areas. For example, regarding my career, I determined that within 10 years of being qualified as a solicitor I would become an associate solicitor within two years, a senior solicitor two years later, then a partner three years later. I also determined how achieving those specific goals would make me feel. I imagined having achieved them even before I did. I resolved to do it. It moved from a wish to a desire. A passion. I managed to smash all those goals ahead of time! It wasn't a stroll in the park, but I had the requisite commitment, the passion, and the drive to make it happen. So, it happened.

Numerous studies show that those who write down their goals achieve significantly more than those who don't write them down. This is noteworthy because writing down your goals engages both the right and the left hemispheres of your brain. Just thinking or daydreaming about your goals uses only the right side of your brain: the imaginative side. If you think about your goals, then write them, you also utilise the left hemisphere, which is the logic-based side. You then get the best of both worlds. That can only be a positive thing!

Needless to say, there's a huge gap between goal setting and goal achievement.   Committing your goals to writing helps narrow that gap.

Be specific, be ambitious, and above all be realistic. We have all heard of setting SMART (**S**pecific, **M**easurable, **A**chievable, **R**ealistic, with a **T**imescale) goals. That's important. Do that. However, your goals must be results focused, not activity focused. The result must be a result YOU desire. It must be personal to YOU.

In setting your goals, start with the end in mind. This means starting with a clear understanding of where you want to end. Your destination. It means knowing where you're going. Knowing where you are right now helps as a starting point. This will enable you to work out where it is you want to get to and to take steps in the right direction towards your property goals.

With goals, you are one step closer to mapping out a pathway to making those dreams into a reality and achieving financial success through profitable property investment.

Mapping out your property goals can be likened to mapping out your journey. Suppose you want to arrive at a specific location in London. Say, Finsbury Park. A map of Finsbury Park would be a great help to you in reaching your destination. What if you're given the wrong map? Say, through a printing error the map labelled "Finsbury Park" was actually a map of Chapeltown in Leeds!

Can you imagine the confusion, frustration, and ineffectiveness of trying to reach your destination? Working on your behaviour and positive thinking wouldn't work in that scenario. It wouldn't make much of a difference, you would still be in Chapeltown. You could try walking faster, deep thinking, being more diligent, or even double your speed. But your efforts would only succeed in getting you to the wrong place faster. You still wouldn't get to the right place.
The point is, you'd still be lost.

The fundamental problem has nothing to do with your behaviour or your attitude. It has everything to do with having a wrong map. If you have the right map of Finsbury Park, then walking faster may help you get to your destination. The right attitude, positive thinking, and diligence in those circumstances would help. The first and most important requirement is having the correct map.

In relation to your property goals, what is your desired destination? What do you want to achieve? Do you have a map of where you are going? Is it the correct map?

By knowing your goals, you can drastically strengthen your ability to make conscious decisions to work towards your goals.

Without goals, your ideas are just dreams. Property dreams.

Goal setting

My short-term property goals

....
....
....
....
....
....
....
....

My long-term property goals

....
....
....
....
....
....
....
....

Checklist

Have you written down your goals?

Are they personal to you?

What does achieving these goals mean to you?

Have you committed to them (verbally, mentally and emotionally)?

Have you made them SMART?

Specific / Measurable / Achievable / Realistic / Timed

Have you placed them somewhere visible?

PO
WER
WITHIN!

"

Determine to change your circumstances. The power is within you.
- *Julie Condliffe*

"

Mindset matters

I invested for independence
Victim mentality wasn't an option.

My unenviable background coupled with my powerful belief system is what has led me to become "a powerful force in the property industry." I am a successful property litigation solicitor and a partner in a law practice, and now have a portfolio that is several properties strong. My goal has been to not only empower myself through successful investment but also to empower others. I have gone through so much on my journey, and I am now passionate about helping people who believe it is impossible. I want to empower you to believe. Even when faced with difficulties, it's holding onto this belief and remembering the lesson of looking beyond the circumstances that have enabled me to persevere and succeed.

Get your mindset right

To be a successful property investor, knowledge about property and certain investment techniques and strategies is critical. However, it is just as important, if not more important, to have the right mindset. To prosper through property, you must develop a prosperity consciousness. A winning mindset.

It starts right between your ears. In your mind. Your

mindset is key. You need to be financially successful in your thinking first long before it manifests in your circumstances.

Growing up in the shantytowns – deep in the ghetto – where people went (and still do) go to school with no shoes on and barely getting by, I had to elevate my mindset **FAR** beyond my circumstances. I had to understand that MY circumstances do not determine my destiny. I do. My attitude determines my altitude, as Mum would say.

Muhammad Ali is a prime example in this regard. Experts relying on what they called "tales of the tape" determined through a series of physical measurements that Muhammad Ali was not capable of being a great boxer. According to the experts, he was doomed. The "tales of the tape" were a series of physical measurements that included the fighter's fist, reach, chest expansion and weight. Muhammad Ali was, according to their 'analysis,' destined to fail. His background and physiology didn't tick the right boxes. But, somewhat surprisingly, and contrary to their predictions, Muhammad Ali became insanely successful. He is regarded as one of the most significant and celebrated boxers of all times. Why? How?

It was his mindset. He determined that he was the greatest. Before he became the world champion, what did Muhammad Ali say? "I am the greatest." When he became the greatest, what did he say? "I am the greatest. What does he say now when he's no longer the greatest? "I am the greatest."

He was successful in his thinking first before he got to the fighting ring. He paid no mind to the "tales of doom" as I call them. You too can achieve success in your property investment with the right mindset. Regardless of your circumstances. Regardless of whatever tales of doom they have told you. You can. You can do it.

What do you say about yourself? What do you say about where you are now? What do you say about your future? Get real. Get positive. Get the right mindset.

Just own it. If you have been negative, change. If you have been pessimistic, change. Only you can do it. First, own it. Accept it. Then change it. The enemy within is always stronger than the external enemy. We must change our mindset. We must conquer the enemy within.

*Buying a home and investing in property are
two very different things.*

This adjustment in mindset is important, especially for first-time investors. When searching for a new home, it's natural to want to buy with your heart and think with your instinct.

For most of us, the process is ultimately about finding a place that "feels" like home and ticks the boxes on your wishlist. However, when you're acquiring property, you need to take a decidedly less emotional approach. As part of defining your investment goals, you should have an idea of how much money you want to generate either through rental income or the sale of a property (cash flow or capital growth). I recommend properties with both cash flow and potential for capital growth.

To achieve your investment goals, you need to create a strategy that's based not on inviting decor or great schools nearby, but on numbers, numbers, numbers!

Mind over matter, money over mind

Successful investors have an objective mindset.

When it comes to successful property investment, thinking with your heart is an easy way to throw your money away. Today, my portfolio is a lucrative mix of residential and commercial property, but my first property was a complete dud.

I bought an overpriced property right at the peak of the property market, using my emotions instead of my brain. I purchased a property I would have loved to live in; as an investor, you need to remove yourself from the equation and ask yourself – is this a property that tenants would want to live in? As a first timer, however, I was completely taken with a stunning property on a "millionaire" street in Swindon. It had an electric gate, fancy mod cons and a sought-after postcode – all things that would appeal to a homeowner, but that ultimately don't matter to an investor.

Seduced by the flash and flare, I didn't do any proper research into the long-term viability of the property as an investment. I was lured by the guaranteed rent that I was promised. It worked – while the guaranteed rent agreement existed, that is. A year later when the guaranteed rent agreement ended, reality hit. I had to subsidise £500 every month just to cover the rental payments! I still had to cover all the other expenses such as repairs, vacancy periods, agency fees and more.

I bought a liability, not an asset. It is cheaper for you to learn from my mistake.

I learnt my lessons from that investment – steep and costly lessons. As a result, all my other properties are completely different. I use my calculator to think, not my feelings. I do the requisite research first. All potential properties are run through several formulas to ensure that they will continue to generate profit; otherwise, they don't make the cut.It's not worth the hassle. The formulas I use are relatively simple. They are based on a minimum yield of 6%. I discuss how to calculate yield later in the book. Math isn't my strongest point. So, if I can do it, you can.

You should treat property acquisition like a business –

have a plan, a budget and an exit strategy in place before making any decisions...even if it does have a four-car garage!

It's all about the money, money, money!

Don't forget about the price tag. I am sure you want your buy-to-let investment to be profitable. So, you want to ensure the figures stack up. You want to get the best return on investment (ROI).

"Yield" is a yardstick commonly used to determine whether a deal is a good deal. Put simply, you want to calculate your rental income and subtract outgoing costs.

To calculate percentage yield, you could base it on the rental income less other annual costs divided by the value of your investment.

Some of the most common deductible expenses are:

Insurance premiums

Premiums for buildings insurance vary by area, type and size of property. It would be sensible to allow for between 2 and 3% of the rent. For furnished property, allow between another 1 and 4% of the rent depending on the level of furnishing.

Mortgage repayments

Of course, your biggest outlay is going to be your mortgage. That's if you have one. To determine your monthly repayment on an interest only mortgage, you take the amount you are borrowing, multiply it by the interest rate, and divide it by twelve.

Maintenance

You will need to allow a percentage of the rent to cover inevitable maintenance costs. Things break down and need to be maintained over time. The type, age, and condition of the property will determine the levels of repairs and maintenance of the property required.

Replacing fixtures and fittings

10% of the rent each year to replace worn out fixtures, fittings, and furnishings would be a generous amount. This is dependent on the age of the property.

Ground rent and service charges

If the property is leasehold, you'll have to pay these charges. Again, they vary largely from property to property.

Void periods

Void periods are unavoidable. It would be sensible to budget for a month each year when the property is empty.

Letting agency fees

Again, these vary. I pay on average 10%. Some of my clients pay lower than that. Some pay higher – up to at least 15%. For me, it is worth the 10% to leave it in the hands of the experts and to save time.

Yield

So, having deducted all the above costs, if the net rental income is £10,000 and the property cost £200,000, the net rental yield is simply £10,000 divided by £200,000 which equals 0.05 or 5%. I would aim for a minimum net rental yield of at least 6%.

believe!

YOUR BELIEFS ARE THE ONLY LIMITATION.
IF YOU BELIEVE YOU **WILL** SUCCEED **IN**
PROPERTY INVESTMENT, THEN YOU WILL.
IF YOU BELIEVE YOU WON'T, YOU WON'T.
-JULIE CONDLIFFE

Analysis paralysis

So, you set your goals. Your mind is set (right I hope). You have read many books. You may have attended many seminars. What's stopping you from starting your investment journey? Analysis paralysis?

Analysis paralysis or paralysis by analysis self-sabotages an inordinate amount of potential investors. It is the state of over-analysing a situation so that a decision or action is never taken, thereby paralysing the outcome.

I recently read quite an interesting story on this online, it goes:

"One day a frog was sunning himself on a lily pad when a centipede came walking by. The frog was immediately entranced by the centipede's flowing and graceful movement across the pad. He marveled at what an amazing ability the insect had to both times and co-ordinated all of those legs so that the result was so smooth and precise. While he was a great leaper and strong swimmer, the frog couldn't help but feel a little jealous of the centipede's skills. After all, his job was so easy, having to coordinate only two legs and two arms, while the centipede's was so much more complicated, having to balance one hundred.

Hoping to be enlightened by the insect's tremendous skill, the frog said to the centipede: "Dear Sir, I am most impressed by your flowing athleticism and your ability to closely synchronize all those legs of yours. I must admit that I could never coordinate 100 legs the fine way that you do. Would I be out of line if I asked you, how in the world do you do that?"

Hearing the compliment from the frog, the centipede stopped his movement and began to beam with pride. He had never bothered to think about how he moved because it was just something that he did naturally. He replied: "Why thank you sincerely, Mr. Frog. I do appreciate your kind feedback. However, I need to spend a moment thinking about how I move before I can share with you my secrets. But now that you mention it, I must modestly say that my ability to coordinate all of those legs at once is truly an amazing feat."

The centipede then began to think very hard about his hundred legs, the order that he had to move each one in and how he timed these movements so precisely. The more he thought about it, the more he marvelled at his ability. However, the more he thought about it, the more complicated the whole process seemed, and he couldn't quite figure out exactly how he was able to do it.

Then he thought, "Perhaps if I walk a little bit, I can pay very close attention to how I move and then I will be able to answer the frog's question more fully." So he explained his intention to the frog and then got up and began to move. However, no sooner had he taken one or two steps that his legs became entangled in each other and he tripped. Slightly embarrassed, he pulled himself back up and once again set out to try and figure out exactly how he was able to coordinate his movements. Once again, his legs became entangled, and he again fell to the pad.

Now the centipede's embarrassment merged with a growing sense of frustration. How was it even possible that he could trip? He had never once tripped in his life and here he had just tripped twice in a row! He quickly righted himself and tried to figure out how best to regain his balance and coordination. He wondered if he was moving his legs out of sequence, or maybe too fast, or perhaps, too slow. He thought about the order of his movement and whether he should start off with the feet on the left side of his body or the right side. However, the more he thought, the more confused he got. This time, after just one step, he went down hard on his face.

His embarrassment and frustration turned to panic. He began to wonder what might happen if he couldn't ever walk again without falling. He immediately got angry, chiding himself for not being able to do something as basic as walking. However, his frustration and anger did nothing to help him walk. In fact, those feelings seemed to make things much worse. The poor centipede was now an uncoordinated mess, falling all around the lily pad. Meanwhile, the frog looked on in curious amusement. Soon the centipede couldn't even stand up!

He quickly thought about what had gotten him into this mess in the first place and inwardly cursed the frog and his stupid question. He suddenly realised that his self-analysis about walking was the one thing that was preventing him from walking. His anger boiled over, and he yelled at the frog, "With all due respect Mr. Frog, Don't ever ask me how I walk again. I do NOT know how I do it and I don't WANT TO KNOW!" After that he got up without thinking and quickly and smoothly ran off the pad and headed for home.

What is stopping you from moving in the direction of your property goals? Is over analysis paralyzing your progress?

You may be asking yourself questions such as:

What if Brexit has a negative impact on the property market?
What if I don't get a tenant?
What if I have many void periods?
What if there is a property bust?

On the face of it, these could seem like reasonable considerations. In reality, they could be excuses debilitating your progress. Just own it.

When investing in property, it can be quite complicated if you want it to be. It can be overwhelming. You can get into the details and can analyse every last bit and come to the conclusion that it's not right for you. Perhaps it isn't. The financial rewards and independence should help sway you. As you know, no risk, no reward.

Using the above questions as an example, the following answers could apply:

Q. What if Brexit has a negative impact on the property market?
A. What if it doesn't?

Q. What if I don't get a tenant?
A. You will. In the unlikely event that you don't, there are various other strategies that you could implement. You could do simple things such as reviewing your target market/your target tenant; setting a competitive rental price; cosmetic repairs/redecoration; or contact the professionals.

Q. What if I have many void periods?
A. Void periods are unavoidable. It's a fact of investment life. You can help mitigate this by buying in an area with consistent rental demand. Keeping the property in good order. You could try and get good tenants and keep them; plan ahead – advertise early; budget for one month per year void period on each property.

Q. What if there is a property bust?
A. Property investment is a long-term strategy. Britain has a long history of busts and booms. After the night, comes the day. You simply need to prepare for it. Pre-emptively seek advice on how best to do that.

As Richard Branson says, "...any fool can make

something complicated, it is hard to keep things simple."

Some of the most successful investors I know have a big picture outlook on life and their investments in particular. On the other hand, the less successful think in a detailed unproductive way. I frequently see how successful investors do well by looking at the big picture and seeing opportunities while the less successful get lost in detail. This often means all they can see problems. A problem-focussed mentality yields problems. An opportunity-focussed mentality yields. You reap what you sow. You can't plant an apple seed and expect to reap oranges.

Both poverty and riches are the result of a state of mind, particularly in this part of the world.

BE YOU.
BE TRUE.
EVERYONE
ELSE IS TAKEN.
-JULIE CONDLIFFE

Change your thoughts.
Change your life.

Passionate about property

The pension crisis, the pain of working long hours, lack of freedom and a defined ceiling on your salary are reasons to run away from the rat race. One of the most important steps you can take along your road to wealth creation is a change in your mindset. A change in your thinking. This must happen before anything else happens.

Your mind is the difference between success and failure.

How bad do you want it?

Having a goal is great. But that's not enough.

You've got to have passion. Desire. A burning desire to succeed. Visualise your success and make it emotional. Connect to it on a higher level.

Once you have devised your goals and you have the motivation to take action, you simply need to employ the right mindset when implementing the plan. Remember, the mindset of a successful investor is one who thinks with the head, not the heart. It's all about numbers, numbers, numbers. You're not about to get married to the property you're buying. In fact, you're not even going to live there. You need to look at things from a business perspective.

It doesn't matter where you are in life, or where you want to go. Your dreams, goals, and aspirations are all possible. You can be a successful property investor. All it takes is proper planning, taking it one step at a time and conquering the things that are holding you back.

Your mindset matters.

I WIN.
I LOSE.
I LEARN.

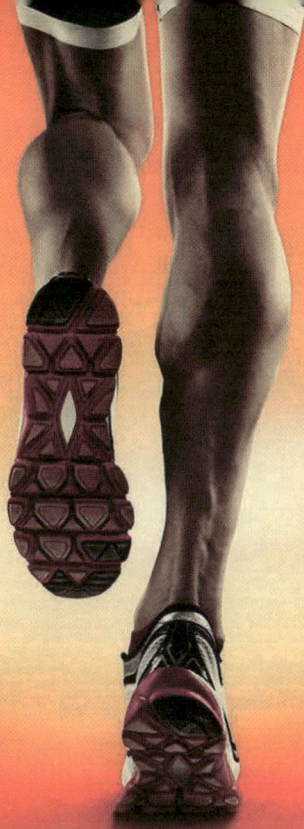

WWW.JULIECONDLIFFE.LIVE

Checklist

Focus on the big picture

Decide to accomplish your goal.

Formulate a set of positive thoughts revolving around your goal.

Develop a step-by-step plan to reach your goal.

Keep a journal of your thoughts and your progress.

Practice getting out of your way.

Be flexible and prepared to start over in the event of setbacks.

See yourself achieving your goal.

Maintain a positive attitude toward your goal.

Do not allow the negative opinions of others to deter you from your path.

Practice daily self-confidence exercises to keep your goal fresh.

Be you. Be true. Just own it.

Strategy

To ensure the successful execution of your plan, it's vital to have a strategic investment approach in place.

There is a myriad of available investment strategies from which to choose, but too many choices often result in confusion and, at most times, bad choices.

The strategy is an individual thing. The best strategy for you will depend on your circumstances and factors such as your attitude to risk, your finances, your plans for management, and your exit strategy. For example, as a full-time solicitor and partner, most of my time during the day is devoted to clients. Therefore, my investment strategy takes a less hands-on approach – I have a team to help me manage my investments so I can still fulfill my work obligations.

For this book, I will focus on two primary types of investment strategy: buy and hold, and flipping.

Buy and hold

With this strategy, an investor acquires a property with the intention of letting it out. This means the property needs to be suitable for tenants and profitable for the landlord. So, research is required into the local rental market before deciding on whether or not to buy. Some investors may choose to buy something that requires some improvements so as to add value to the property, while others prefer something turnkey and move-in ready so as to keep hassle to a minimum. Which you decide is again, dependent on your goals and your lifestyle.

The buy-to-let market has grown and continued to grow. The fact that the UK is experiencing a housing shortage has increased the viability of the buy-to-let market. An increasing population has also led to a shortfall in available properties. As a result, house prices in many areas have risen to unaffordable levels for a lot of people – especially first-time buyers. This has meant that people have been forced to rent instead.

A key thing to keep in mind with this strategy is the amount of ongoing work that will be required. There's a great deal required in terms of property maintenance, keeping up with legislation changes, tenant screening and turnover, and so on. It is possible, even with a full-time job. You just need to be organized. Whether you choose to adopt a hands-on approach to managing your assets or to instruct a property letting and management agency to do so on your behalf is a matter of preference, but if the latter, make sure to account for this in your budget when running your monthly cash flow calculations.

There are quite a few buy-to-let strategies at your disposal.

HMOs

I recommend that you start small. That just means less risk. There is quite a learning curve in investments. You can minimize your mistakes by reading up as much as you can and attending seminars. There are plenty of online forums and events for you to attend.

That said, if you have a single let, you are particularly exposed to the risk of a bad tenant as they represent ALL your property income.

The more adventurous may want to opt for HMOs. An HMO is defined along the lines of:

A building or a part of a building which -

(a)consists of one or more units of living accommodation not consisting of a self-contained flat or flats;
(b)the living accommodation is occupied by persons who do not form a single household;
(c)the living accommodation is occupied by those persons as their only or main residence, or they are to be treated as so occupying it;
(d)their occupation of the living accommodation constitutes the only use of that accommodation;
(e)rents are payable, or another consideration is to be provided in respect of at least one of those persons' occupation of the living accommodation, and

(f)two or more of the households who occupy the living accommodation share one or more basic amenities or the living accommodation is lacking in one or more basic amenities.

Typical HMOs include student houses, a group of friends sharing a house or professionals sharing a house.

The benefits of an HMO are that as you're letting rooms in a single house to some people, the rent they pay will be far greater than a single let. So, they can be a highly profitable investment strategy.

There are, however, quite a few additional regulatory requirements peculiar to HMOs. These include licensing.

Location matters more when it comes to HMOs. Ideally, the property needs to be located close to a city, a town centre or a university. A village or rural area just wouldn't cut it.

Student lets

Students lets are a potentially lucrative investment strategy.

By way of example, I bought a three-bedroomed tenanted property in the Middlesbrough TS1 area. The property was let to a family who was paying a monthly rent of £325,00. I reconfigured the property and converted it to a student let. I now let the property to four students who pay £79 per student per week. The rental income I now achieve weekly (£316) is almost equivalent to the rent I used to achieve monthly. The total annual rent the previous tenant used to pay was £3,900. The total annual rent I now receive is £16,432. A staggering difference of over £12,500! Over a period of 10 years, the total rental income would be £164,320 instead of a meagre £39,000. That's an astounding difference of £125,320!

If this sounds exciting to you, here are some of the things you'll need to consider when making an investment of your own.

First, the location must be right. If you buy a property in a village far out in the sticks with no university close by, it is likely that this strategy would not work for you. You would want to buy a property in a university town. Even then, it would be prudent to ensure the property is within easy walking/cycling distance to the local university.

Second, in light of the high yields, the student market is very competitive. So, properties need to be of a high standard. Be mindful of the initial outlay in this regard. You would want to pay for things such as separate bathroom ensuites, separate kitchenettes, bright and flamboyant décor. The price will vary depending on the location, size of the property and the precise scope of the work involved. You may also want to bear in mind the inevitably greater tenant turnover. Inherently, management costs are likely to be higher.

Third, you'll also need to do your research, or get expert help, so that your letting is structured in line with the HMO licensing regime previously discussed. On the other hand, there is no liability for council tax if the property is occupied by full-time students.

Last, some say student lets are fraught with complexity. Not in my experience. I find that students are far less demanding. Their parents normally pay (on time). The property is vacant over the summer months, allowing you a period to re -let on a short-term basis or to redecorate.

Buy-to-let or Buy-to-regret!

The buy-to -let strategy you choose to adopt is your prerogative, just be mindful that if not managed properly, it could turn into a buy-to-regret.

You must ask yourself a series of questions. Do you have sufficient capital at your disposal? Are you happy to tie up this capital for some years? Buy to let is a long-term investment. Have you the resources to manage the property?

If the answer to any of these is no, then it's not worth getting involved. However, if you're still keen to proceed, then you need to do your research. Be realistic about how much you can afford, remembering to have cash to cover unexpected costs and for periods when the property is empty.

There are overt circumstances that could make one buy-to-regret or regret using this strategy. The most obvious ones are things such as void periods. We discussed ways to reduce the impact of void periods above. Knowing your market and investing with a target tenant in mind does help.

Being faced with a non-paying tenant is a situation no landlord wants to find themselves in. If you take the right steps, it need not turn into a nightmare. Initially, you could adopt a less adversarial stance by talking to your tenant to get to the bottom of the cause. It may just be a temporary resolvable situation. If the conciliatory approach is unfruitful, you could contact the guarantor or take various legal steps to recover the arrears.

There are clear pros and cons about getting involved in buy-to-let. Anyone considering going down this route will have to weigh these up carefully before committing their time and money.

Wealth without debt

What if I told you there was a strategy to make money

from property without having bought a property?

Lease options allow you to become wealthy without getting into serious debt. They enable you to get into the property game with little or no money. They are a remarkable strategy giving you wealth without debt.
This is welcome news for anyone who is not mortgageable or anyone without enough money for a deposit. This could also work for someone with available funds, but who simply wants to leverage and upscale.

The lease option strategy can help you make thousands of pounds in a very short period.

How do you define a lease option?

It is easier to define what a lease is, then define what an option is.

A loose definition of a lease is that it is a legally binding agreement by which one party gives to another, property, land, building, equipment, vehicle(s) or services for a specified time in return for a periodic payment.

An option can be defined as a right, but not an obligation, to buy or sell the underlying asset (which in this case will be subject property).

There are two ways of using Lease options. One is a

lease to buy (rent to buy), and the other is a lease to rent (rent to rent).

The first strategy, rent to buy, allows you to rent the property now and buy it when you are ready. You buy a house for a defined price in the future. You will, in the interim, enjoy the benefits of being a landlord including the rental income.

The option agreement can be for any agreed period. It can be as long as ten or fifteen years. During that period, you will have the flexibility of choosing your ideal finance, at the ideal time, and at the ideal rate. In the interim, you will simply rent the property.

Entering into an option agreement is pretty straightforward. You simply need to agree proposed terms with the landlord. An easy – and indeed commonly used – way to kickstart that process is by agreeing on heads of terms. These are the key points outlining each party's requirements. The document doesn't have to be all-singing, all dancing. A few simple bullet points will suffice. You simply need to outline:

- The parties' details
- The property details
- The deposit payable
- Monthly/quarterly fee payable
- Proposed purchase price
- Lease length term

- Liability for property maintenance

This document will help the solicitors in drafting the legally binding documentation.

Allow me to share with you two examples of lease options in my portfolio. One is a rent to rent, the other is a rent to buy.

Rent to Rent

The property is in Coventry. I rent it from a landlord and then rent it out for more money. The figures for that particular property are as follows:

Tenant pays monthly rent	£1,910.00
I pay landlord	£865.00
Utilities	£350.00
Monthly profit	**£695.00**
Annual profit	**£8,340.00**

The landlord, in this case, was struggling to keep up after his acrimonious marriage breakdown. We will use "Mr. Jones" as a pseudonym for the landlord by way of protecting his identity.

The property had been vacant as it hosted painful memories for poor Mr. Jones. He did not want to sell the property. Not immediately anyway. He wanted to keep the property but needed the peace of mind of knowing that the mortgage will be paid. He was emotionally battered and did not have the capacity to deal with the added burden of managing the property.

I offered Mr Jones the peace of mind of ensuring that the mortgage was paid every month by giving him guaranteed rent. I took away the burden of managing the property.

I vividly remember Mr. Jones said to me "Julie you are the miracle that I have been praying for."
My eyes welled up with tears. This is what I always wanted. Helping people is my passion.

At the end of the option period – depending on his circumstances –Mr Jones will have the following options:

1. To continue with the lease option
2. To sell the property
3. To take back his property

All options are available to him.

Mr. Jones was a victim of his circumstances. We helped him turn his situation around by helping him achieve everything he wanted.

This deed gave me a powerful positive spark. That feel good factor. It also helped me profit from my passion in property. Win-win for Mr. Jones and I.

I would recommend always looking for scenarios where everyone benefits. It is in helping others that we benefit the most.

Rent-to-buy example

This relates to a property in London.

Tenants pay monthly rent	£6,077.00
I pay landlord monthly	£1,900.00
Monthly gross profit	£4,177.00
Annual gross profit	**£50,124.00**

Impressive figures! We must, however, consider the costs expended in reconfiguring the property for which I obtained the requisite licences from the landlord for. The utilities are an additional cost. These are one-off costs, which will quickly make money back.

As the lease length terms are 15 years, we agreed on a rent review at year five of the term. The landlord also gave an option to purchase the Property during the term of the lease at an agreed price of £700,000. Some lease options provide the purchase price as being the open market rent. I wanted a degree of certainty.

Options are versatile. At the end of the option period, you have an option to either buy the property or just hand it back. You are under no obligation to keep the property. It is a win-win situation.

Property values are likely to increase within that option period. So, you would benefit from the capital appreciation.

The landlord does not have as much flexibility, with his obligation to keep the option open for you for the duration of the option period.

You have control and profit from a property without the burden of ownership.

Fix and flip

I'm sure you've heard about property flipping. You've probably seen it on Homes Under the Hammer and other similar television programmes.

Property flipping is defined as buying and selling a property within a short period. It often involves repair and renovation of the property in order to realise the maximum sale value achievable.

If you don't want the hassle of holding onto property, you may wish to buy below market value, do up the property, and sell it for a profit.

There are some variables that contribute to the success of this strategy, but if done well, investors can stand to see a sizable profit upon completion. You'll need to consider things such as how much time you have to renovate, and of course, how much money you want to invest.

You could buy a property that is substantially below market value and in want of cosmetic repairs. The scope of the work involved may simply entail applying a lick of paint or just updating the visual appeal of the property and put it back on the market for a quick resell. Or it may be that you buy a property that is in need of substantial repairs.

Either way, having a complete and thorough home survey carried out is vital, as this will alert you to structural issues. Working with an experienced surveyor will ensure that you make a good investment, so you avoid buying a property with issues that are dangerous and costly to repair. It is just a matter of doing your due diligence.

Things to consider to ensure you get it right:

Understand what buyers demand in the marketplace and what they're willing to pay for.

It's important to do your research to ensure that you can sell your property and capitalize on all your hard work. Before embarking on your property hunt, start looking for properties to flip; you must first understand who your buyer is and what they are looking for. If you provide homes that meet your target buyer's needs and perhaps wants, you will give yourself the competitive edge to demand higher sell prices.

For example, if your target buyer is a family, make sure your properties are in a safe area close to schools and parks. Property that is close to public transportation and other amenities such as dining and shopping are likely to appeal to a wider market.

Understand your investment area

It's essential to research what's going on locally so that you're not shooting blind. This ensures that you're making a sound investment that you'll be delighted with rather than having regrets later. You want to know where the market activity is coming from. You also want to know whether there are any proposed developments in the area.

Ensuring that the property is located in a strategic area close to hospitals, recreational places, and other important amenities is a prerequisite.

The property

As we have already discussed, buying investment properties is all about the bottom line – making you money.

So, you want to buy below market value property then

sell at the top of the market value. To achieve this, consider buying from:

A motivated seller (a person who is compelled to sell a property often at below market value because of economic circumstances; a relationship breakdown; probate issues or some other reason.

Retiring landlord

Repossession

Dilapidated properties below market value

Accurately price repairs or else. You can do this by obtaining three comparison quotes. It can be an uphill task to accurately project renovation costs.

You also need a realistic after repair valuation (ARV). Your flipping success hinges on the resale value of the property.

If possible, find a buyer before you complete!

To be "flipping" successful, you need to be able to:

Identify a goldmine of income-generating property in want of repair.

Start with a specific business plan in mind. Include a

timetable outlining timescales for each stage of the flip. A budget for each flipping stage will be invaluable. You may want to consider the type of properties you want to buy; how much profit you want to make, and how many deals you want to make annually.

Purchase the property at a profitable price.

Factor in realistic timescales (taking into account potential delays).

Get an accurate estimation of the renovation costs.

Stage the property (almost like a show home).

Study and understand the market.

Know your target buyer and what the buyer wants.

Know how to calculate profitability.

Understand how to measure the ARV.

Questions to ask yourself

When trying to decide upon your investment strategy, you may want to consider the following questions as a starting point:

1. How much time are you able to devote?

Tip: If you are planning to manage a property portfolio whilst also doing your day job, then you may want to consider a joint venture or hiring a property manager.

....

....

....

2. Are you able to set yourself apart from others with a website and online marketing strategy?

....

....

....

3. How comfortable are you cold-calling and reaching out to find deals?

....

....

....

3.1. Or would you rather search for deals online or instruct an estate agent for help?

....

....

....

4. Are you comfortable with negotiating?

....
....
....

5. Does the area around you fit with your property investment goals and ideal target market?

- *Are buyers young families, working professionals or retirees?*
- *What neighbourhood would appeal to which buying groups?*
- *What type of home is each buying category interested in?*

....
....
....
....
....
....

5.1. Are you able to go further afield?
Tip: *It may be that the area near you is more suited to family homes, but you want to invest in student accommodation.*

....
....
....

6. How much risk are you willing to take?

....
....
....

7. Are your property investment goals short-term or long-term?
Tip: *If you're looking for short-term capital gain, then flipping houses at auctions or a property development is more suited to you.*

⁄ ....
....
....

8. Are you looking to save for retirement?
Tip: *If your goals are more long term then your strategy should focus on low-risk buy-to-let properties.*

....
....
....

Once you have answered these, you are in a better position to start putting your plans into place.

Flipping properties can be a lucrative investment strategy. Focus on your primary goal. That is, earning a profit by buying a property below market value and selling it at a premium.

IDENTIFY YOUR MOUNTAIN.
SPEAK TO IT.
DON'T DOUBT.
IT WILL MOVE.

WWW.JULIECONDLIFFE.LIVE

Sourcing

Once you have determined your strategy, it's time to start thinking about where to find your chosen properties!

I am often asked about how best to go about finding a property that is a guaranteed "good deal," and the truth is there are some places you can begin a property search. With that said, more than 90 percent of property searches in the UK now begin online.

Online portals such as Right move and Zoopla are great places to start; you can see local and nationwide listings, along with information such as past sale prices, the number of days on the market, average market conditions, Energy Performance Certificates and more. These properties are known as being "on market," meaning they are publicly listed as being advertised for sale. Once you've spotted a listing you like, you can contact an estate agent for more information. Of course, the more traditional property buyer with a soft spot for bricks and mortar may begin his or her search in a high street estate agency anyway!

How do you spot a listing?

Many investors will look for properties that are off the market, too. There are some reasons people may not want to advertise a property for sale – perhaps the family home is being sold due to a relationship breakdown, and some discretion is required, or maybe they have inherited a property from a deceased loved one and want the sale of it handled quickly and with privacy. In cases such as these, sellers are often keen for a quick sale, which can mean they'll accept offers below market value – already a great start for investors! To source these deals, you can look at visiting property auctions, or attend investor networking events. You could even direct market specific neighborhoods with flyers through the door to see if anyone is thinking about selling in a hurry. Never hurts to be proactive, right?

Sourcing companies

Sourcing companies specialise in finding properties and passing them on to investors for a fee.

Depending on your personal circumstances, this could be a viable option for you. It could save you a lot of time. The key thing to bear in mind is not every deal presented is a good deal. Trust, but validate.

Estate Agents

Regardless of what people say about them, estate agents are my friends. They help alert me to potential hot deals before the deals are published. They are my primary sourcing agents.

I suggest you make friends with estate agents in your chosen investment location. It will help you.

What makes a "good deal"?

A successful investor knows how to spot property investment trends and translate them to their goals.

The property must be right. It has to be profitable. Successful investment is about return on investment. This could be capital appreciation over the long term or rental return more immediately. Ideally, you want a combination of the two.

Location matters.

You may be tempted to choose somewhere close to you out of sheer convenience. However, if your local market doesn't have the right fundamentals in place, this could be a huge mistake. Currently, the North West of England – Manchester in particular – is the most lucrative area in the UK to invest in property for those seeking high rental yields with no shortage of demand. A specific example of this is Salford, Greater Manchester, which had the highest proportion of households renting socially at 35.3%. You also have the opportunity to earn an average yield of 6.15% in Manchester, the highest city according to the BTL Index. Up and coming areas for high rental yields are Stevenage, Coventry, and Romford. At the bottom of the list are Galashiels, Western Central London, and Llandrindod Wells.

It won't surprise you that London and the South East of England are reported to have the highest annualised return. Properties in London generate an annual return of 7.9%, and Cambridge properties generate 5.99%. Due to the high house prices in these areas, the rental market does not perform as well as the North of England so choose London or the South East of England if you are looking to generate high capital gains from your investment.

Ultimately, it comes down to how much you are willing to invest, what type of mortgage you are looking to get, the amount of risk you can take, and whether you are looking for it to be a joint venture.

Investing in a non-local area

If the place where you want to invest is not where you live, it would be wise to do some research on the area. Equally, if you've never been there before, I would suggest you obtain a general knowledge of the town to get a good understanding of what the place is like.

With technological advancement, you could go for a virtual walk around the street using Google Street view. This will allow you to see a panoramic 3-D view of the street. You can use the directional keys to wander around the locality.

A good understanding of the area would help you know where you should invest in that particular town. Every town has good parts and bad parts. You can find a lovely property in a practical location, but if it's in the roughest part of town with no amenities close by, then this could affect your ability to rent the property. You can only make money if someone pays you!

I remember earlier on in my investment journey, I bought a "show home standard" three-bedroomed property in Wellingborough. I lived at least 50 miles away. I knew nothing, or very little, about the area. To a novice, the potential rental yield was attractive; so was the purchase price. On the face of it, it ticked the boxes.

I had not carried out any real detailed research about the area. I relied heavily on what the selling agents communicated to me. Not a smart move. The property was an ex-council property. Not that there is anything wrong with that per se. However, I later found out that that particular estate has a reputation for being the worst council estate in the county! Wellingborough does have a lot of beautiful areas. Finding a tenant was like finding a needle in a haystack. I found myself in an unattractive set of circumstances. Or did I put myself there? Whichever way, it was unenviable. I had to ride the storm and later managed to sell it at a heavily discounted price. I made a loss.

Research is crucial. If you're not able to do the research, keep it local. Investing locally cuts down on travel costs and enables you to utilise your local network. You will know the good and bad areas in your local area.

Sometimes it's better the devil you know.

In choosing to invest non-locally, you may want to consider investing in:

1. An area with good transport links
2. A seaside town
3. An area with planned developments
4. University town
5. Big cities

This is not, by any stretch of the imagination, an exhaustive list. It is simply a general guide.

Prize the process.
Trust the process.
Allow it.

Acquisition

*Found the ideal property that meets all your criteria
and passes all your financial tests? Great!
Now it's time to buy it.*

It's understandable at this point – especially if you are a first-time investor –that your imagination may run away with you a little. While buying a property can be an exciting time, it's important to map out your acquisition strategy as part of your overall plan so as not to make any careless mistakes. Take your time. It is a process.

Like I said earlier, you're not buying a home, but making an investment, so your plans for acquisition should be as sound as the rest of your investment strategy. For example, do you plan to buy one at a time, or mass purchase? Is the property leasehold or freehold? Are you acquiring an HMO, and if so, are there any stipulations about which you should be aware?

Once you've answered these questions, then it comes to enacting your plans to finance the deal. There are a few ways you can do this as an investor, a few of which are outlined below.

BTL Mortgages

Britain's buy-to-let boom has seen some mortgage

providers offer financial products specifically for rental properties. In this instance, meeting with your bank or mortgage advisor is the first step to acquiring the property. They'll be able to advise you on the types of mortgage available so you can determine which is best for you. Remember, your monthly sum less expenses should cover the cost of your mortgage payments and still provide some left over for you as profit.

Paying With Cash

More experienced investors who have already made a profit and have a cash sum available may choose to buy a property outright using this money. There are many benefits to this – you can often buy quicker and be a more attractive bidder to sellers, and you don't have to waste time and invest energy into paperwork applying for a mortgage.

Before making an offer, meet with your accountant or bank advisor to ensure that there won't be any unexpected repercussions and get their opinion on how much you can afford. Once you have your budget, then contact the sellers and negotiate on the price. Another benefit of being a cash buyer is you may have some negotiating power – if you are acquiring a property that has been on the market for a long time or is in an unsaleable condition, you may be able to lower the price. Similarly, if the sellers are in a hurry, as cash purchase is faster, they may be inclined to accept a lower value.

Joint Venture

The two most common types of partnerships in investing in property are equity partners (those who pay in cash) and finance partners (those who take a loan out from the bank). It is critical that you ensure that you and your partner have similar goals for the property and each of you is in a financial situation to pay your share. For many, a joint venture can be very lucrative. For those who fail to do their due diligence, however, it can be a story straight from a horror movie. Where many of these cases have fallen are that there was not the correct written agreement between the parties. You, therefore, need to have a lawyer such as myself create a legal joint venture agreement that is signed by all parties. This is the sort of thing I have regularly been doing to clients for over ten years now. The fee is a small sum to pay compared to the profits you'll be making from the property overall.

YOU ARE
AN OVERCOMER.
YOU'VE GOT THIS.

Renovation

By updating the property before letting, you can command higher rental rates and potentially appeal to a more affluent tenant demographic.

If you are purchasing the property with the intention of flipping, doing it up will already be part of your business plan. I am asked often how much I should spend renovating a property. There are rules of thumb out there that you can follow that will give you a percentage to spend on each room depending on the valuation of the property. Although this is a good starting point, you should focus on what your property needs. You may also want to consider the average sale price of similar houses in the local area, along with the average rental rates if you're looking to let. This will help you avoid overspending on renovations in comparison with the market; after all, you are looking to make a profit and should approach renovations with a business mind to make a healthy profit on the property.

Get the basics right to add value to the property.

It is your job to make the property look like a place that a stranger could make their home. Get a contractor in to ensure that the work is done to a high quality, and cover your cash flow by ensuring there is a written agreement about what will be done, when, and how it will be paid.

Focus on getting the kitchen and bathrooms to a high standard. The kitchen is the most valuable room in a home per square footage, and so it is often the easiest way to add value. Clean, modern bathrooms are always in demand too, so this room should be your next area of focus. Ideally, you want the property to be appealing to your target demographic, so consider who is looking to rent or buy in that area when approaching your renovations. For example, a younger demographic in want of a modern home may appreciate little additions such as up-to-date power outlets – you can install plug sockets alongside iPhone charging points throughout the property, for example.

Little touches like keeping the colour scheme neutral and making the hallway look presentable will help to boost first impressions. Hire a gardener to make sure that the front garden looks tidy and welcoming and that the back garden is well-kept. For extra points, have planning permission for an extension/basement or transform the front garden to have space for a car.

Management

"If you want to go fast, go on your own.
If you want to go far, go together."

When it comes to managing a property portfolio, creating a strong and reliable team is of the utmost importance. Hiring a property manager is quite common; if the property manager is good and within your budget, then they are worth their weight in gold. Make sure you screen your property manager thoroughly before you hire them, to ensure you get someone who is good at their job and a gem that you'll treasure. This will save you time and trouble later on down the line. Either way, there are some checks and legalities that you will need to have in place for your new property.

Be honest about what needs to be done

Consider how much time you have to devote to asset management and whether you need to hire someone to help you.

It can sometimes feel overwhelming to be managing one property alone, let alone more. The rewards make it worth the time, money, and effort ... but you also want to stay sane while you're doing it and have time for your family. You may, therefore, want to hire someone to help you. For some people, being hands-on is a must –

and that's OK! Others feel more comfortable leaving the ongoing management of a property in the hands of a professional. Whichever you choose is ultimately up to you, but you may wish to start by understanding the fundamentals of what needs to be done:

- All legal checks need to be carried out by up to date landlord and tenant laws.
- All properties need to have EPC and gas certificates secured.
- All tenants must undergo complete reference checks and screening.
- Rental agreements must be written up, signed and filed. In the tenant contract, outline who is responsible and liable for the various ways of maintaining the property.
- Deposits need to be collected, secured and returned at the end of the tenancy.
- Monthly rent needs to be collected.
- Emergency call-outs will happen, so have access to a list of tradesmen who are reliable, efficient, and able to react quickly in case of emergency call outs for repairs. They will become a valuable member of your team and will help to keep your tenant happy, encouraging them to stay in the contract.
- Have a point of contact, whether it be yourself or a property manager, who can respond quickly to any queries from the tenants.
- Search around to get the best deal on insurance for the property in case of damage. You are looking for

an insurance policy that protects you from financial losses connected to your rental property, commonly associated with damage and theft.

Ask yourself whether you will be able to manage this yourself and whether you have the skills to do so. You may be tempted to cut costs and do this all yourself, but there's more to property management than just the price. Consider the demands on your time along with your skill set and desired amount of effort, and decide whether or not you would be better off doing it yourself.

Celebrate your uniqueness!

You were not created to fit in. You're too great to fit in a box.

Conclusion

Property investment has the potential to be a lucrative and enjoyable process.

For me, investing has helped me gain not only a tangible passion for something but also a great deal of experience that has helped me realise my life goals. I've gone from sleeping in a phone booth to managing a portfolio of multiple properties that generate cash flow enough so that I can live comfortably – achieving the goal my mother had for us.

I had no idea what I was doing when I got started. I hated evicting tenants and was nervous about buying at auctions. It all seemed scary and daunting, and I was nervous what could go wrong. But if I had my time over, I'd have got started sooner. It changed my life. If I can do it, you can too.

I wish you all the best with your property journey, and hope the lessons and tips contained in this book will help you achieve new levels of success and personal fulfillment!

You are the change you have been praying for.

Take Action»

In Summary

Have clear, attainable goals from the outset.

Create a financial formula and test the viability of all assets before buying.

Purchase with purpose – don't buy based on emotion! You're not buying a home; you're making an investment.

Be creative when sourcing your deals.

Be realistic when financing them.

Don't skip steps to save time or secure a quick deal – missing any structural issues can result in costly and time-consuming repairs that could compromise the viability of your investment entirely.

Have an exit strategy, and ideally a backup plan.

Consider your property management costs and demands for your time – can you handle the investment yourself, or is it worth enlisting professional asset management? If the latter, make sure to include the cost of this in your calculations.

Julie Condliffe – The Legal Diva

Affectionately known as 'The Legal Diva,' Julie is a property investor with over 10 years experience. She is also a specialist property litigation and dispute resolution solicitor with over 15 years property law experience. She is genuinely passionate about property. She is poised to help you maximise your investment and turn your property passion into profit.

Professional Experience

As a property investor, she knows and understands the challenges faced by landlords. As a dispute resolution solicitor, she helps landlords resolve disputes on a daily basis. She spends a significant amount of time in court fighting and winning landlords' battles. As a landlord, she has the hands-on knowledge of how best to maximise your investment. As a property litigator, she knows which battles to fight successfully and which to avoid. So, whether at the negotiating table, in the courtroom or before a tribunal, you will be alongside someone with an extraordinary track record of success.

Julie draws upon her extensive experience, trusted judgment and insight to help you develop a customised strategy to manage your investment and save you time and money. Julie understands that landlords want to avoid rent void periods, recover arrears cost effectively and speedily, and that they want to steer clear of expensive and protracted evictions. Julie can help you, and your landlord tackles these challenges efficiently and effectively so that you can move ahead.

Freebies!!

I would love to help you in every step of your property investment journey.

So, please connect with me on social media or just email me at Julie.Condliffe@outlook.com.

Register (for free) using Julie.Condliffe@outlook.com to receive:-

* Regular updates on all things property

* Step-by-step guide on how to start your investment journey

* Guidance on how to get mortgage ready

* How to determine the value of a property

It's all completely free. No gimmicks. Just email: Julie.Condliffe@outlook.com

Leave a review on Amazon for your chance to receive a FREE strategy session worth £250.

Have any questions?

Get in touch, and I'll answer them on my podcast, The Property Pro Show.